Anger Management

Advice For Women On Handling Anger In Relationships And Preventing Fights That Can Ruin Your Happily Ever After

(Instruments For Overcoming Angry Feelings And Keeping A Healthy Emotional Balance)

AlkiviadisKatsanos

TABLE OF CONTENT

Emotional Intelligence Refers To The Ability To Perceive, Understand, And Manage One's Own Emotions, As Well As To Recognize And Empath..................1

The Causes And Effects Of Anger..................10

Acquiring The Skill Of Diplomatic Communication: An Exploration Of Assertiveness Training..................14

Make The Determination To Never Retire For The Night While Experiencing Feelings Of Anger..................19

The Utilization Of Cognitive Behavioral Therapy (Cbt)..................51

The Prevailing Physiological Indicators Of Anger..................57

The Topic Of Discussion Pertains To The Formative Period Of An Individual's Life, Commonly Referred To As Childhood And Upbringing..................76

Reconsidering Perspectives On Life..................89

Postpone The Manifestation Of Emotional Anger..................103

Theory Of Interactionism 116
Tips For Maintaining Healthy Relationships And Managing Anger 123

Emotional Intelligence Refers To The Ability To Perceive, Understand, And Manage One's Own Emotions, As Well As To Recognize And Empath

Emotional intelligence, often known as EQ, refers to the capacity of an individual to accurately perceive and effectively regulate their own emotions, as well as the emotions of others. Depending on the specific manifestation of anger, individuals may discover that it is highly advantageous not only for anger management purposes, but also for gaining insight into the cognitive distortions caused by anger and for exploring other methods of expressing underlying concerns.

In a comprehensive perspective, there exist four primary dimensions of emotional intelligence (EQ) that necessitate your attention in order to effectively manage and regulate anger in a definitive manner.

The first pillar of focus in this context is self-awareness.

Undoubtedly, self-awareness stands as the fundamental element among all parts of emotional intelligence (EQ), since its absence renders one incapable of comprehending their fury, let alone identifying the most probable factors that incite it. The ability to engage in introspection and evaluate one's own qualities and attributes is crucial for personal growth and development. Without this capacity, it becomes challenging to make progress and enhance oneself.

The second pillar of focus is self-regulation.

Self-regulation is considered to be an inherent progression of self-awareness. When an individual achieves a comprehensive understanding of their own experiences, it becomes significantly more feasible to effectively manage and control areas of concern that may have previously been overlooked or disregarded. Enhancing one's self-regulation abilities facilitates the comprehension of personal anger triggers and enables proactive preparation for anticipated trigger-inducing circumstances.

Self-regulation pertains to the cognitive process of considering one's actions before executing them. This ability is closely linked to self-awareness, as heightened awareness of one's typical mental state facilitates the detection of deviations from the norm. Although it may provide challenges to refrain from expressing anger by negative means, consistent effort will reveal that it is comparatively simpler to disengage from such inclinations. Ultimately, enhancing one's self-regulation skills might facilitate the ability to empathize with the other party, thereby potentially defusing the situation from the outset.

The third pillar of this framework pertains to motivation.

Individuals possessing a high emotional intelligence quotient (EQ) exhibit a propensity for motivation due to their comprehensive comprehension of the multiple mechanisms through which cognitive processes impact behavioral outcomes. To enhance one's ability to manage anger effectively, it may be beneficial to establish personal goals that strike a balance between being challenging enough to need effort, yet attainable enough to avoid appearing insurmountable. This approach can serve as a catalyst for initiating the process, particularly when lacking the necessary drive.

The fourth pillar of consideration in this context is empathy.

Empathy is a crucial element of emotional intelligence (EQ) as it enhances one's ability to comprehend and appreciate the emotions experienced by others. By developing a deeper knowledge of others' emotions, individuals are less likely to react with anger towards them. Moreover, this heightened empathy often facilitates the discovery of resolutions that do not elicit feelings of wrath within oneself. Enhancing one's empathy might facilitate the avoidance of making judgments towards both others and oneself. Enhancing one's empathy does not require any hidden or elusive strategies; rather, it necessitates a conscious endeavor to comprehend the perspective of others. Although individuals may not always share the same perspective, fostering a receptive mindset can facilitate the identification of shared interests or beliefs with nearly any individual.

The concept of triggers

Enhancing one's emotional intelligence (EQ) through focused efforts on the four fundamental pillars might facilitate the identification of triggers that lead to the loss of rationality and succumbing to rage. Individuals possess triggers, which can be either external or internal stimuli that override rational thinking and prompt instinctual behavior. Fortunately, enhancing one's self-awareness and self-control not only facilitates the identification of personal triggers but also facilitates the modification of subsequent responses when these triggers are activated.

Guidelines for Appropriate Behavior

One should acquire the ability to recognize the indications, manifestations, and consequences of rage. In order to effectively address one's anger issues, it is imperative to accurately identify and recognize them. A significant portion of individuals lack awareness of their condition due to a lack of knowledge regarding the nature and characteristics of the problem. It is commonly believed that the absence of overt expressions of frustration may indicate the absence of anger. However, it is important to recognize the existence of latent anger, which can be more perilous than its confrontational counterpart. It is advisable to acquire knowledge on the many manifestations of rage in order to ascertain if professional assistance is required.

Channel your frustration into a productive and useful manner. A considerable number of individuals tend to commit the error of repressing or concealing their anger, however, this does not align with the principles of anger management. The act of repressing one's anger does not lead to its dissipation, but rather contributes to its internal accumulation. It is imperative to acknowledge and articulate feelings of rage, yet in a non-destructive manner. This is the fundamental aspect. Engaging in physical aggression towards an individual who has provoked one's anger is evidently devoid of constructive or beneficial attributes. Conversely, adopting a proactive approach to address and resolve both the immediate anger and the underlying factors is undeniably more advantageous. Identify the source of one's anger and its underlying causes, thereafter undertaking proactive measures to address and resolve these concerns.

It is advisable to actively pursue the assistance that is required. Anger issues are classified as mental health concerns, thus necessitating the pursuit and acceptance of assistance in order to effectively address and overcome them. The phenomenon of anger extends beyond mere displays of irritability and excessive use of profanity in moments of distress. Its detrimental effects can permeate several aspects of an individual's life and well-being, encompassing physical, mental, and emotional dimensions. One should not underestimate the potentially detrimental impact of one's emotions, as doing so may result in experiencing adverse outcomes.

The Causes And Effects Of Anger

When experiencing anger, individuals often tend to immediately assume that they comprehend the underlying cause. The individual is experiencing anger due to perceiving a negative facial expression directed at them. How frequently have you encountered or engaged in a dialogue in which one individual inquires, "What is the reason for your anger?" while the other party responds, "I am simply experiencing it"? Individuals may experience this sentiment on occasion, nevertheless it is imperative to recognize that there is invariably an underlying factor that propels this arduous emotional state.

The primary factor contributing to individuals' tendency to deny is the inherent difficulty associated with managing and processing these complex emotions. The aforementioned obstacles will persistently manifest themselves, necessitating our active engagement and resolution in order to achieve a state of increased happiness and well-being. Failure to effectively manage one's anger can lead to a multitude of adverse consequences that have the potential to significantly disrupt one's life and result in long-lasting harm.

The experience of anger is often accompanied with an underlying cause that may not be immediately apparent. The exploration of the underlying factors contributing to anger was briefly introduced in the preceding chapter, and will be further examined in this subsequent chapter.

At times, individuals may be so deeply influenced by their emotions that they have difficulty in discerning the underlying cause for their emotional state. The greater our willingness to explore the veracity of our emotional condition, the more effortless it will be to ascertain the genuine foundation of this sentiment.

Next, we shall examine the impacts of rage. At certain instances, it is conceivable that they may align with our interests, candidly speaking. It is possible that an individual exhibited a strong emotional reaction when the idea of having tacos for dinner was proposed by others, leading to a collective decision to acquiesce and unanimously opt for pasta as an alternative choice. On that particular evening, we successfully obtained our desired outcome. Simultaneously, it is important to acknowledge that our chosen response in that particular situation has the potential to undermine the perspectives formulated by others. The transient nature of rage necessitates an examination of its immediate consequences, while also acknowledging its enduring impact that surpasses the temporal duration of the emotional experience.

In addition, it is important to acknowledge that rage can give rise to a multitude of significantly consequential health concerns. Due to the nature of chemical reactions, there exists a significant probability for it to commence exerting an influence on the total physiological chemistry within the human body. The intensity of one's anger can disrupt hormonal equilibrium, which is undesirable due to its influence on emotional states.

When an individual experiences hormonal imbalances, it becomes imperative to promptly address and rectify the issue. Frequently, it entails mitigating the levels of stress and worry that individuals encounter. The topic of anger will be discussed in chapter 4; however, it is essential to examine the fundamental origin and indisputable consequences of anger in our daily existence (Potegal, 2010).

Acquiring The Skill Of Diplomatic Communication: An Exploration Of Assertiveness Training

Engaging in a conversation with the one responsible for the source of irritation and expressing one's dissatisfaction has the potential to rekindle the previously experienced feelings of anger. Despite individuals acquiring the ability to manage their anger in the absence of the offending party, they often have difficulties in effectively expressing their displeasure when confronted face-to-face with that individual. Assertiveness training is incorporated into anger management interventions within this particular environment.

What are the distinctions between assertiveness and aggression?

Both of these concepts pertain to the act of conveying one's thoughts and emotions to another individual. However, these distinctions can be discerned by directing attention to one particular aspect:

Aggression is predicated upon the desire to achieve victory, as it is intrinsically linked to the imperative of survival. Consequently, their sole objective is to manipulate the circumstances to their advantage, disregarding the well-being of others. Failing to consider the well-being of others will not lead to any favorable outcomes.

The concept of assertion is rooted in equilibrium, as individuals who exhibit assertiveness prioritize effective communication of their own desires and requirements, while simultaneously taking into account the desires and requirements of others. Individuals may not attain their desired outcomes, however they find satisfaction in the compromises they are able to achieve.

How can one cultivate assertiveness?

To cultivate proficiency in communication, it is important to implement the subsequent procedures:

The concept of self-worth and the recognition of one's own rights

An one who possesses assertiveness should acknowledge that their own rights, beliefs, and feelings hold equal value to those of others, without being deemed superior or inferior. In order to safeguard one's own rights, it is imperative to undertake appropriate measures for their defense. Similarly, it is not always necessary to offer apologies when one has committed an error. In order to foster effective communication, it is imperative to not only seek understanding from others but also to ensure that one's own thoughts and ideas are comprehensible to others.

It is important to maintain a respectful demeanor, especially when communicating feelings of rage.

Acquire the skills necessary to effectively express emotions in an assertive and tactful manner. By employing this approach, it will signal to the other party your genuine commitment to encouraging a modification in their conduct. By expressing one's dissatisfaction with a particular action rather than directing criticism at the individual responsible, it is possible to minimize the likelihood of the recipient taking offense. Consequently, this approach fosters an environment conducive to collaborative problem-solving, wherein both parties are motivated to find a mutually beneficial resolution.

Make The Determination To Never Retire For The Night While Experiencing Feelings Of Anger.

According to the biblical passage found in Ephesians 4:27, it is advised not to allow anger to persist until the end of the day, as doing so may provide an opportunity for the devil to gain influence or control. Engaging in sleep while harboring feelings of anger might be considered a form of defiance against divine authority. The aforementioned factors can potentially disrupt our sleep patterns, render us vulnerable to spiritual attacks, and compromise our physical well-being.

Make a commitment to refrain from subjecting oneself to such distress. It is advisable to proactively address any instances of anger that may have arisen throughout the course of the day. Subsequently, entrust individuals whom you perceive as beyond your capacity to manage to the divine being through supplication, beseeching for the purification of your mental and spiritual faculties.

10. Engage in a constructive dialogue regarding one's experience of rage with family members and loved ones.

Misunderstandings often arise due to inadequate communication. It is conceivable that rage has produced a substantial rift between oneself and one's family members or friends. It is advisable to initiate conversations with family members and close acquaintances regarding targeted strategies aimed at enhancing the quality of interpersonal bonds with each individual.

In the event that anger has exerted an influence on one's interpersonal connections, it is advisable to engage in mutual apologies, engage in joint prayer, discern constructive measures that each individual can undertake to restore the relationship, and subsequently proceed with the implementation of those measures.

11. Acquire the ability to effectively address and rectify misinterpretations in a prudent manner.

In reality, despite using various strategies to manage anger, individuals will inevitably face numerous instances of disagreements, misunderstandings, and minor altercations, necessitating astute handling in order to derive favorable outcomes from such situations. When confronted with disagreements, it is advisable to abstain from reacting with wrath towards the words or actions of others. Instead, it is advisable to maintain a state of attentive silence until the individual has concluded their verbal expression. Subsequently, it is imperative to ascertain one's role within the conflict and beseech divine intervention in order to effectively articulate one's thoughts with a demeanor characterized by benevolence and deference.

Acquire knowledge through the experience of battle and implement any necessary modifications guided by divine influence based on the lessons assimilated.

Day 9: Understanding Your Triggers

Each individual possesses a trigger, a specific stimulus that has the potential to incite a strong emotional response, subsequently leading to the manifestation of problematic outcomes. The individuals in question may have been functioning adequately until a specific stimulus prompts them to experience emotions such as anger, frustration, or distress. Frequently, individuals experience a loss of self-regulation due to the overwhelming influence of their emotions, leading to subsequent actions that are later met with feelings of remorse. Developing proficiency in identifying emotional triggers is a crucial aspect of enhancing one's emotional intelligence. By acquiring this talent, individuals can effectively mitigate or confront these triggers, thereby maintaining emotional regulation.

Individuals possess several triggers that elicit emotional responses. The occurrence of anger or outbursts directed against those in one's immediate vicinity cannot be attributed to random chance.

For a significant number of individuals, rage triggers are often associated with circumstances that are linked to certain sources of stress or feelings of insecurity. Individuals experiencing high levels of stress in various domains of their lives, such as work, home, or other contexts, are prone to exhibiting heightened reactivity towards even minor inconveniences due to reaching a state of emotional and psychological saturation. However, is it fair to cause harm and inflict negative emotions upon others due to one's own little stressors? Acquiring the knowledge and skills necessary to effectively regulate and minimize one's stress levels represents a highly advantageous course of action under the present circumstances.

If the presence of personal insecurities is contributing to the emergence of challenges, it may be necessary to address and resolve the underlying factors responsible for their existence within one's life. The occurrence of unpleasant remarks or constructive criticism in a professional setting does not provide a valid justification for responding with explosive outbursts or engaging in aggressive or inappropriate behavior. Acquiring the skills to effectively manage one's insecurities, as well as identifying their underlying causes, can significantly impact one's interpersonal responses.

Numerous stimuli might incite individuals to exhibit impulsive behavior during heightened emotional states; yet, it is imperative for individuals to assume responsibility for regulating their emotions, regardless of the circumstances. Gaining an understanding of the specific stimuli that elicit emotional responses and promptly addressing them will facilitate the regulation of one's emotions, so preventing their undue influence on one's daily existence.

When experiencing emotions of anger and distress, it is advisable to pause momentarily and engage in introspection. Is it justifiable for one to experience such emotions at the present moment? In the event of a reaction, regardless of its justifiability, will one have a sense of satisfaction upon its completion? What other methods can be employed to express frustration or discontent without causing harm or engaging in any form of unkind behavior?

I would like to inquire about the introspective process about the experience of emotion, specifically in terms of its validity. Is it plausible to ascertain whether an individual's anger or hostility towards oneself is genuine, or may it be attributed to one's own disposition on a given day? I can assist you in recognizing that acting upon one's emotions may not provide commensurate benefits in light of the subsequent emotional repercussions. Indeed, there exist instances wherein one's feelings are justified; nonetheless, even under such circumstances, it is imperative for individuals to maintain agency and not allow their emotions to dictate their actions.

Furthermore, it is advisable to commence the practice of documenting your triggers for a consecutive week in the future. If an individual consistently encounters a multitude of triggers that surpass their capacity to effectively monitor during a given day, it is advisable to commence by addressing the three most significant triggers on a daily basis. It is recommended to proceed by assigning a severity rating to each item on a scale ranging from 1 to 10. Ultimately, it is imperative to acknowledge and document the coping mechanisms that one is presently employing, irrespective of their positive or negative nature.

After assigning labels to all the triggers, it is advisable to arrange them in a sequential manner, commencing with the least intense and progressing towards the triggers that elicit profound wrath even from a considerable distance. After generating your list, in the event that you were unable to formulate a list that sequentially commences at one and extends to ten, it is advisable to engage in thoughtful contemplation and make an earnest attempt to identify stimuli that would adequately populate the entire scale. By systematically addressing each trigger, one can gradually escalate the intensity of rage experienced with each episode, thereby preventing the inadvertent undertaking of overwhelming emotional burdens.

When engaging in this exercise, it is of utmost importance to proceed at a deliberate pace, ensuring that you transition to the subsequent trigger only after achieving a state of experiencing the preceding trigger without any apprehension or concern. It is imperative to adhere to a sequential approach when addressing each item on your list, since deviating from this order will not expedite the resolution of your concerns and may, in fact, impede progress by introducing the emotional burden of an additional setback.

Recommendation #4: Visit a location that holds personal significance to you.

Is there not a location that we hold great affection for? Is there a destination that has always piqued our interest, although remained elusive due to time constraints? Alternatively, the small village in where we experienced some of the most serene moments throughout our formative years. Alternatively, could you maybe provide information regarding the beach that we visited during our honeymoon? This location belongs to you.

Experiencing feelings of anger? Please proceed to the designated location promptly. There is no requirement for a ticket, luggage, or itinerary. Instead, one might envision oneself engaging in a game of football in a location previously frequented during adolescence, or alternatively, standing at a beach where a romantic week was spent with a significant other. Rather than simply affirming your presence, endeavor to mentally recreate the location with precision, either as you recall it or as you desire it to be.

Recall all facets of the location, encompassing auditory stimuli, olfactory sensations, atmospheric conditions, and meteorological patterns. Remain in your current location until such time as you have fully depleted all residual fury that was previously experienced, and subsequently return. The sound produced is a rapid movement of air. The entirety of your fury has dissipated.

Tip #5: Document the information

Are you experiencing intense feelings of hostility or a desire to cause harm to others? Have you ever contemplated the hypothetical scenario of being able to expeditiously remove a someone from a building by means of forcibly propelling them from the twelfth level, thereby effectively terminating any further interaction or engagement with this individual? It is not feasible to engage in such behavior, regardless of the intensity of one's anger towards an individual.

One such action that can be undertaken is to transcribe the information into paper or another suitable medium. Please retrieve a writing instrument and a sheet of paper, and commence the act of making hasty and disorderly marks: I possess a strong aversion towards that individual. I express a desire to terminate his/her existence. The individual in question is causing significant distress and hardship in my life. I express a desire for negative consequences to befall them. I harbor strong negative sentiments towards him/her. I express a strong desire to avoid encountering him/her in any future circumstances.

Please transcribe all the statements that you envision expressing to that individual. Once the individual's anger has subsided, proceed to dispose of the document. The objective is to prevent any individual from ever perceiving it. Ultimately, the emotions experienced in this context are not reflective of genuine sentiment, but rather a manifestation of one's rage. The assertions made in your written statements regarding that individual appear to lack sincerity or genuine intent.

One may attempt to articulate their emotions through written expression; nevertheless, employing analog methods proves to be the most effective approach for releasing feelings of fury.

Tip #6: Cultivating Trust in an Individual

It is highly likely that there exists an individual within your own network who possesses a strong inclination to provide assistance and support during this particular endeavor. During a critical juncture, seek their attention to assist in achieving a state of tranquility.

When experiencing feelings of anger and frustration while waiting in a queue, individuals may choose to contact the relevant authorities and express their dissatisfaction, potentially resorting to complaining or expressing their discontent in a vocal manner, such as by stating, "This situation is highly frustrating!" I have been waiting in line for more than an hour. I find it disconcerting when my supervisor appropriates all the recognition for my contributions. I desire to take action in response to the situation.

If an individual is genuinely concerned for one's well-being, they would exhibit a patient tolerance towards any expressions of rage. It is more advisable to express frustration or anger towards individuals who have provoked such emotions, rather than directing them onto innocent bystanders in a wait or one's superior at work.

Suggestion #7: Incorporate Humor

One commonly known technique in public speaking is the visualization of the audience members in a state of undress as a means to alleviate stage fright. This has resemblance to the aforementioned concept.

When faced with a source of anger, it is advisable to employ humor as a coping mechanism. When experiencing frustration towards one's supervisor who is reprimanding one's team, one may envision the supervisor adorned in a clown's costume, complete with a prominent rubber nose. This will enhance the situation by envisioning a clown vociferating towards oneself. It is important to exercise caution and refrain from openly expressing amusement in the presence of one's supervisor, as such behavior may have negative consequences for one's professional standing.

Engaging in these seemingly little activities can assist individuals in effectively regulating their anger for brief durations. It is crucial to bear in mind that acquiring the ability to regulate anger in the immediate term can facilitate a broader perspective and ultimately serve as a guiding force in navigating one's challenges. The ability to effectively manage anger at its first stages is indicative of the potential to eventually achieve perfect control over it.

There appears to be a widely acknowledged consensus that it is preferable to refrain from expressing anger in the context of our increasingly socially advancing society. Anger is commonly perceived by society as an emotion that diminishes our capacity for rationality, relegating us to a state of instinctual behavior. Consequently, it is widely acknowledged that such a circumstance should be diligently circumvented. However unattractive rage may appear or feel, it is important to acknowledge that it is a legitimate emotion and an inherent aspect of human existence, akin to other emotional states. In essence, there exist certain phenomena within our universe that have the capacity to induce a state of unhappiness within individuals, to the extent that it may provoke feelings of anger.

However, it is important to note that even although fits of wrath may seem justifiable, they are not excusable. When anger is not effectively regulated, it has the potential to do significant harm. The phenomenon exacerbates the situation and engenders further negative consequences beyond the initial problem that ostensibly triggers anger.

In the immediate timeframe, exhibiting anger does not contribute positively to any given circumstance. At its most optimal, this behavior only instills fear in individuals and compels them to respond defensively or with counter-aggression. However, it fails to elicit genuine cooperation from individuals.

Over an extended duration, it has detrimental effects on interpersonal connections. In the absence of a shared comprehension and subsequent reconciliation, the aforementioned instance of anger has the potential to negatively impact the perception of individuals involved, hence potentially damaging one's reputation.

Established and deliberate outrage

The expression of settled and intentional anger might be a response to the perception of highly conscious malevolence or unjust treatment inflicted by others. This type of challenge is characterized by its indirect nature.

The concept of dispositional wonder refers to an individual's innate inclination or tendency to experience a sense of awe, curiosity, and fascination

Dispositional amazement is more frequently attributed to the formation of character rather than to sensory experiences or perceptions. Immovability, dismalness, and brutishness are indicative of the ultimate phenomenon.

The factors that contribute to or bring about a particular phenomenon or event.

Shock is a commonly seen physiological and psychological reaction that individuals experience in response to various threatening or hazardous situations. Perseverance is greatly influenced by the presence of vexation. The experience of shock can manifest as a challenge when one is unable to effectively manage it, leading to the expression of negative emotions or engaging in regrettable actions. A recent study suggests that inadequate self-control has detrimental effects on both physical and mental well-being. Moreover, it will rapidly escalate to verbal or physical aggression, affecting both yourself and individuals in your vicinity. Various factors can serve as catalysts for mental acuity, such as the burden of responsibilities, familial challenges, and financial difficulties. For several individuals, curiosity is experienced as a significant drawback, akin to addiction to alcohol or feelings of despair. Shock is not universally regarded as problematic; yet, the manifestation of astonishment can serve as a notable indicator of some circumstances.

The following are some of the plausible factors contributing to the phenomenon of wonder.

The concept of wretchedness refers to a state of extreme unhappiness or suffering experienced by

Instances of outrage are frequently depicted as a visual representation of despondency, characterized by prolonged feelings of sadness and a diminished sense of motivation lasting for a minimum duration of two weeks. Instances of outrage are frequently suppressed or overtly expressed. The intensity of the public's anger and the methods through which it is expressed vary from individual to individual. Individuals experiencing melancholy may exhibit certain symptoms. The aforementioned factors encompass: • heightened sensitivity • decrease in energy levels • feelings of melancholy • Challenges pertaining to self-harm or self-destructive behavior

The phenomenon of fanatical normal problems refers to instances where individuals exhibit excessive and unwavering enthusiasm or devotion towards mundane or ordinary matters, often leading to disruptive or problematic outcomes

Obsessive-compulsive disorder (OCD) is a psychiatric disorder characterized by intrusive thoughts and compulsive behaviors. Individuals diagnosed with Obsessive-Compulsive Disorder (OCD) experience distressing and unwanted thoughts, emotions, or images that compel them to engage in repetitive and meticulous behaviors. For example, individuals may engage in specific rituals, such as counting to a certain number or repeating a word or phrase, due to an irrational belief that something negative would occur if they fail to do so. According to a recent article, it has been suggested that anger could be a common symptom of Obsessive-Compulsive Disorder (OCD). Approximately 50% of individuals diagnosed with Obsessive-

Compulsive Disorder (OCD) are affected by this phenomenon. Outrage can arise as a consequence of feelings of powerlessness in preventing obsessive thoughts and compulsive behaviors, as well as interference with one's capacity to engage in a routine.

An Analysis of Different Forms of Anger

The following are the several classifications of rage:

Borderline Personality Disorder (BPD) is a mental health condition characterized by a pervasive pattern of instability in interpersonal relationships, self-image

This particular manifestation of anger is commonly observed in individuals diagnosed with borderline personality disorder, a psychological condition characterized by a pervasive sense of rejection or unacceptance. The primary sign of this particular disease is the inability to regulate emotions.

An individual exhibiting such a form of intense anger may lack awareness of abrupt shifts in their emotional state. For example, individuals may experience a shift in emotional states, transitioning from happiness to anger within a short span of time. Individuals afflicted with borderline rage frequently exhibit a tendency to distance themselves from their significant others due to a prevailing belief that these individuals may perhaps abandon them in subsequent instances. Individuals retrospectively evaluate their behaviors and frequently experience a sense of regret, potentially resulting in the development of depressive symptoms.

The term "narcissist" refers to an individual who exhibits excessive self-adm

In the context of narcissism, individuals manifest a form of anger wherein they perceive a threat to their self-esteem, leading to the expression of wrath. This phenomenon may present itself as unmanageable rage, resulting in instances of physical violence. Individuals who exhibit such intense anger have a propensity to intentionally do harm to others.

Bipolar disorder is a mental health condition characterized by extreme shifts in mood, energy levels

Bipolar disorder has the potential to manifest a distinct and individualized manifestation of intense anger. Individuals diagnosed with bipolar illness experience a cyclic pattern characterized by alternating episodes of mania and depression. Mania engenders a sense of empowerment and optimism, occasionally leading individuals to become disconnected from reality. Individuals in this context may exhibit impulsive tendencies and have a persistent stream of racing thoughts. Individuals experiencing a manic condition may exhibit aggressive conduct and expressions of wrath, often without a conscious understanding of the underlying cause.

As previously stated, individuals are consistently subject to various stimuli that elicit feelings of anger, with the specific triggers differing among individuals. Nevertheless, there exist some fundamental categories of stimuli that might elicit feelings of rage.

The Etiology of Anger

Several commonly seen reasons of anger are evident in the majority of individuals. By acquiring a deeper understanding of these underlying factors, we can enhance our comprehension of rage.

The Existence of Unmet Needs as a Potential Threat to Safety

Every individual has distinct essential requirements that are necessary for their well-being and contentment. The fundamental necessities encompass sustenance, hydration, habitation, repose, protection, and wellbeing. When individuals' fundamental needs are not met, they may encounter feelings of wrath. This rage arises as a consequence of the arduous efforts required to fulfill basic survival requirements. The duration of deprivation directly correlates with the increasing level of desperation to satisfy those wants.

The experience of rage in individuals is frequently attributed to the presence of unfulfilled demands and perceived risks to personal safety. Unfulfilled needs can lead to feelings of frustration and emotional distress. Unfulfilled wants encompass the experience of inadequate feelings of affection or acceptance.

The topic of grief and loss is a significant area of study within the field of psychology. It encompasses the emotional and psychological responses that individuals experience when they encounter the death of

Grief is an inherent emotional response that manifests at the loss of a cherished someone or the anticipation of an impending loss. suffering is an inherent aspect of human existence, and it is permissible to experience sensations of suffering. Nevertheless, the dominance of grief in one's life can render them susceptible to vulnerability. The experience of losing a cherished individual is profoundly agonizing and does not readily dissipate.

Anger is considered to be one of the stages within the grief process. Experiencing anger at that particular instance is deemed acceptable. Individuals may have a sense of powerlessness, leading them to question many aspects of their lives that contribute to feelings of helplessness.

Anger may also manifest due to feelings of abandonment resulting from the departure of a loved one, leading to a profound sense of emptiness in one's life. Another contributing cause to this manifestation of fury is the incapacity to come to terms with the loss of our beloved one. Sadness and dread are other elements that contribute to the experience of rage in relation to loss.

The Utilization Of Cognitive Behavioral Therapy (Cbt)

Cognitive Behavioral Therapy (CBT) has been extensively employed as a therapeutic approach for managing repetitive occurrences of uncontrolled anger or flare-ups, as well as anxiety attacks. It is imperative to refrain from suppressing feelings of anger and anxiety, and instead, acquire the necessary skills to effectively manage and channel these emotions in a manner that yields positive outcomes.

Cognitive Behavioral Therapy (CBT) is a therapeutic approach that combines cognitive and behavioral techniques to address psychological distress and promote positive behavioral change.

This form of psychotherapy facilitates the recognition and

understanding of the detrimental cognitions and consequences associated with one's expression of anger, with the guidance and support of a trained psychotherapist. This is achieved through a sequence of sessions that serve the following objectives.

Please identify the stimuli that trigger your episodes of anger and anxiety attacks.

Identify the cognitive distortions associated with anger outbursts and episodes of anxiety.

Acquiring the skill of transforming negative thoughts into positive thoughts amidst these episodes of distress.

Under the professional guidance of a counselor or psychotherapist, individuals have the opportunity to acquire alternative positive behaviors that can effectively replace negative ones, thereby facilitating the appropriate management of anger. It is important to acknowledge that the process involves not suppressing anger, but rather redirecting the associated emotions towards outcomes that are more advantageous.

In the workplace, individuals may experience feelings of anger and anxiety due to perceived instances of condescension from their colleagues.

Rather than resorting to outbursts or aggression, individuals can effectively channel their anger or frustration towards personal growth. This can be achieved by engaging in activities such as enhancing public speaking abilities, expanding knowledge through reading, acquiring social interaction skills, and striving for overall self-improvement. By undertaking these endeavors, individuals can cultivate self-confidence and advance various facets of their lives. The individual's emotional energy has been reallocated towards personal growth and self-improvement. All the outcomes have positive implications for you. Undoubtedly, individuals who previously diminished your worth would now hold admiration for the accomplishments you have attained.

The individual is experiencing a state of anger, anxiety, and stress as a result of another person disseminating a rumor regarding their lack of honesty.

In this particular case, the problem is approached in a direct manner, characterized by a calm demeanor. In the context of one's professional responsibilities, it is imperative to address any misconceptions by providing substantiating evidence that demonstrates one's adherence to ethical conduct in their employment. Such evidence may include transaction records, receipts, testimonies from witnesses, and similar forms of documentation. Expressing anger may lead others to perceive you as being culpable. In the event that one is unable to substantiate their honesty, it is advisable to adopt a posture of indifference and strive to enhance one's attentiveness towards their actions. It is advisable to maintain comprehensive documentation of your transactions and, to the greatest extent feasible, ensure the presence of a corroborating witness.

These illustrative instances would enable individuals to adopt a proactive approach, channeling their energy towards constructive actions rather than solely expressing anger, which may result in subsequent remorse over the inflicted harm.

One may consider engaging in Cognitive Behavioral Therapy (CBT) with limited therapist involvement. This phenomenon is potentially feasible. It is imperative to refrain from engaging in negative conduct when experiencing feelings of anger and anxiety. Maintain a log documenting instances of anger and anxiety, while also recording corresponding responses. By redirecting one's emotional energy from feelings of anxiety and anger towards constructive behaviors, individuals may experience a reduction in the frequency and intensity of anger outbursts and anxiety attacks. One would develop a calm disposition.

The Prevailing Physiological Indicators Of Anger

Acute stress, anger, and anger-provoking events are recognized as significant stressors for the human body. Upon their occurrence, the sympathetic nervous system is activated as a result of hormone release. The sympathetic nervous system elicits the activation of the adrenal glands, leading to the secretion of adrenaline and noradrenaline. Consequently, there is an elevation in heart rate, blood pressure, and respiratory rate. Following the cessation of the threat, the body will require a duration ranging from 20 to 60 minutes to restore its physiological state to the levels observed prior to arousal. As a consequence of this hormonal alteration, a notable observation will frequently be the elevation of one's heart rate.

The individual may experience a reduction in visual field.

The muscles have the potential to experience increased tension.

The individual may experience the onset of perspiration.

One potential effect is an increase in auditory sensitivity.

These physiological changes are a result of adaptive mechanisms that facilitate the fight or flight response.

• Enhanced sensory perception: The redistribution of blood flow restricts peripheral circulation, thereby augmenting blood supply to the upper extremities, lower extremities, shoulder girdle, cerebral region, ocular structures, auditory organs, and nasal cavity. In addition to preparing for physical exertion and combat, the human body undergoes cognitive adaptations to facilitate rapid thinking and heightened vigilance, enhancing auditory, visual, and olfactory perception of potential threats.

Sweating is a physiological response characterized by the secretion of sweat from the sweat glands, which serves to regulate body temperature. Engaging in activities that require a high level of exertion can lead to an elevation in body heat, consequently triggering the process of sweating. In anticipation of such circumstances, the human body initiates perspiration upon perceiving stress, thereby facilitating thermoregulation.

Dilated pupils serve the purpose of allowing increased light intake, thereby enhancing visual acuity.

Dry mouth occurs as a result of reduced production of gastric juices and saliva due to a decrease in blood flow to the digestive system. This discussion pertains to the concept of prioritization within a given timeframe. Prioritizing survival in the present moment takes precedence over the process of digesting food. This particular physiological response can also induce gastrointestinal discomfort in the immediate period, and when activated, frequently leads to persistent gastric distress.

Various physiological responses of the sympathetic nervous system can elicit discernible alterations in posture or movement, such as heightened respiration, clenched fists, dilated nostrils, pacing, or elevated vocal intensity during speech.

When an individual experiences anger, their physiological response is geared towards mobilizing resources to effectively respond to a perceived threat in order to ensure their survival. In a scenario resembling a wilderness setting, wherein an individual is evading pursuit by a bear, the human body undergoes a series of physiological responses aimed at facilitating survival. However, given the shift from a natural habitat to a domesticated environment, individuals possess the capacity to regulate these developed responses. This enables them to regain a certain level of authority and ascertain the distinction between a genuine bear encounter and emotions such as rage or annoyance that do not pose a direct threat to their well-being.

The act of expressing anger is a common phenomenon observed in human behavior. It is a manifestation of strong negative emotions that can arise from

When examining the matter of anger management at its core, the fundamental question that arises is: How can we effectively communicate and manifest our anger in a manner that is conducive to our overall well-being? The experience of anger is characterized by physiological reactions associated with the fight or flight response, as well as the cognitive and emotional manifestations that it elicits within our psyche. Anger can be described as a formidable source of energy characterized by its propensity for action. The occurrence of this phenomenon is inherently natural. The phenomenon under consideration cannot simply vanish, despite our desire for it to do so; rather, it necessitates expression.

When the fight or flight response is activated, the body will execute the actions dictated by this response, irrespective of the influence of rational cognition. Hence, the significance of our mindfulness expedition cannot be overstated. The concept of mindfulness entails a continuous and proactive choice to anticipate and regulate the manifestation of anger, so enabling individuals to exert control over their emotional expression. One rationale for engaging in this practice is to acknowledge and uphold the regularity of the emotion, while remaining cognizant of its practical purpose. Boundary establishing and safety are being facilitated by this phenomenon, which serves as a source of energy and support for both ourselves and others.

Anger exhibits a significant functional aspect when experienced. At what point does it transition into a state of dysfunctionality? The observed phenomenon can be attributed to a persistent absence of attention, wherein the uncontrolled expression of rage within our physiological system is permitted. For a significant portion of individuals, the occurrence of an angry body response is repeatedly activated, preventing the retention of memory information related to the event in the long-term memory. Consequently, the ability to access, comprehend, and acknowledge the event as a previous experience is hindered. The experience of rage can become entrenched into the neurobiological structures of the brain and body, leading to a tendency for individuals to react in a similar manner when encountering novel events that bear resemblance, either in outward or interior aspects. This process establishes a network of interconnected responses characterized by rage, which perpetually strengthen one another. The experience of discomfort gives rise to a necessity to either release the accumulated energy through physical activity or resort to actions and cognitive strategies aimed at desensitizing the individual. This is the point at which the manifestation of rage becomes maladaptive. Once more, the issue at hand is not the emotion of rage. The present analysis pertains to the subjective perspective on anger, specifically when it is manifested in a manner that surpasses the individual's genuine requirements, evades emotional experiences through substance abuse or behavioral patterns, and/or inflicts harm upon oneself or others.

The topic of discussion pertains to domestic abuse.

Typically, we have the opportunity to observe the profound impact of abuse on individuals, yet we often choose not to intervene due to a perceived lack of personal relevance or an excessive valuation of our own priorities. The maximum extent of your perceived capability is to provide guidance. Despite the veracity and continued efficacy of this approach, I would consider implementing a more noticeable gesture to express both your concern for the well-being of the affected party and your willingness to provide them with the necessary assistance they truly require. In contemporary discourse, it is common to express concerns over interpersonal relationships, familial dynamics, or societal issues. However, it is worth considering a shift towards converting these concerns into constructive endeavors. Attempt to emulate the actions and behaviors that we advocate for, and witness the transformative potential of extending a second chance to another individual via the unique capabilities of your hands.

The identification of an individual engaging in abusive behavior

There are several factors that arise as to why individuals choose not to engage in mediation, primarily due to the victim's reluctance to allow intervention, as the abuser often employs a familiar pattern to manipulate the victim's rationality. The individual engaging in abusive behavior will transition from a very hurtful and ruthless demeanor to a conciliatory stance, accompanied by purportedly earnest assurances of change. This temporary respite, however, proves insufficiently enduring as the abuser inevitably reverts back to their cyclical pattern of abusive activity. It is advisable to intervene in a deliberate and premeditated manner, rather than spontaneously, by formulating a comprehensive plan and subsequently taking action when all necessary conditions are in place to ensure the safety of the individual in question. Typically, individuals tend to overlook instances of abuse due to the perpetrator's adeptness in presenting a composed and amiable demeanor in public, which often leads others to perceive them as considerate or incapable of causing harm. Identifying the identity of an abuser can provide challenges, often relying on the victim's portrayal of abuse symptoms for accurate identification. It is important to avoid allowing the perpetrator's seemingly kind actions and morally culpable intentions to justify their actions. When the silence is shattered and the victim separates from their abuser, the abuser will employ all means necessary to portray themselves as a virtuous individual. The perpetrator may exhibit signs of distress, despair, and sadness, and may even attempt to shift blame onto the victim for their own actions, thereby seeking validation for their behavior. Occasionally, the narratives they recount appear rational, especially if they have recently exhibited acts of kindness and generosity towards you. In authentic situations following the departure of the victim from the abuser, the abuser may endeavor to establish friendly relationships with the victim's acquaintances or relatives in an effort to maintain proximity to the victim's social circle and gather information. Various persons may engage in errors, however, in the context of a domestic violence case, these abusers escalate their actions to a more severe offense. It is not only a mistake if their harmful behaviors persist on a daily basis over an extended period, significantly impacting the well-being of another individual. That behavior cannot be avoided.

Maintain a positive outlook.

Negativity possesses the capacity to dominate one's cognitive processes. Persistent negative thinking can contribute to a decline in mood and then result in the manifestation of emotional outbursts. If you find yourself surrounded by negative people, consider distancing yourself from them. The significance of the negativity within one's mind extends beyond its mere presence. The presence of negativity within one's surroundings holds equal significance.

The human experience encompasses both moments of triumph and moments of adversity.

It is important to acknowledge that experiencing both positive and negative circumstances is a common occurrence throughout the course of one's life. The phenomenon of experiencing this rollercoaster is not exclusive to any individual, but rather a shared occurrence among all individuals. Recognizing the normalcy of one's experiences can contribute to emotional regulation.

In certain situations, adopting a passive stance can prove to be the most effective course of action.

One could get a sense of being trapped within a certain circumstance. There is no feasible course of action to improve the situation. Occasionally, this phenomenon does occur. Observe the natural progression and ascertain the resultant consequences when refraining from intervention. Furthermore, it is imperative to refrain from engaging in any actions that may exacerbate the current circumstances. Engaging in impulsive decision-making is typically unproductive and has the potential to exacerbate one's circumstances.

It is advisable to refrain from becoming excessively critical of oneself.

It seems probable that individuals tend to be their own worst critics. Demonstrating self-compassion is of utmost importance. It is important to bear in mind that diligent efforts are being made to effect substantial alterations. It is advisable to grant oneself a respite when errors are committed. It should be acknowledged that the task of effectively managing one's high emotions is a challenging endeavor, and the mere act of endeavoring to initiate this shift is commendable.

Effectively managing one's emotions is a crucial aspect in addressing and coping with feelings of rage. It is possible to observe that individuals may also experience other emotions with equal intensity during episodes of acute rage. The attainment of complete emotional control remains an elusive objective. It is advisable to experiment with several methodologies until a suitable one is identified. The source of information may comprise a combination of the options proposed in the above list, or it may stem from other scholarly investigations that have been conducted. A crucial aspect in the process of treating one's emotions is taking ownership of one's sentiments. Acknowledging one's emotions, regardless of their positive or negative nature, constitutes the initial phase in realizing the acceptability of experiencing anger, sadness, or happiness.

Consider this perspective: The resolution of a leaky pipe necessitates the prior identification of the puddles present on the floor.

The Topic Of Discussion Pertains To The Formative Period Of An Individual's Life, Commonly Referred To As Childhood And Upbringing.

A significant number of individuals were socialized within an atmosphere that instilled in them the belief that frequent displays of anger and aggression are acceptable and typical behaviors. Individuals exhibit diverse strategies for managing anger, although certain individuals have not been adequately instructed in the acquisition of anger coping mechanisms. During childhood, certain individuals may have been socialized with the belief that expressing rage is permissible under any circumstances. They were raised in an environment where they did not acquire the necessary skills to comprehend and effectively regulate their feelings of rage. Individuals tend to react with anger in response to any perceived aggressive or unfriendly circumstances due to the habitual nature of this behavioral response. Numerous individuals were socialized to adhere to the belief that irrespective of circumstances, they should consistently suppress their wrath and refrain from its outward manifestation. This particular group of individuals likely had disciplinary measures during their childhood due to their tendency to display emotional outbursts. Over time, they acquired the ability to restrain their anger, even in situations where they may have preferred to express it. The consequence of this phenomenon is that individuals of this nature consistently exhibit incorrect reactions when confronted with situations that challenge their feelings of safety and contentment. For instance, a someone who has been socialized to inhibit their expression of rage will refrain from outwardly manifesting their wrath, even in response to actions or behaviors that they find displeasing. However, it is inevitable that at some point, he would experience fatigue from suppressing his emotions, leading to a potential outburst of fury in response to a scenario that may not warrant such a strong emotional reaction. Consequently, this portrayal renders him as exhibiting irrational and inappropriate behavior. This is why it is neither advantageous to suppress one's anger nor to express it excessively. Furthermore, a significant number of individuals were raised in an atmosphere characterized by the constant presence of adults exhibiting anger, so exerting an influence on their own personality development as they internalize the belief that anger is an acceptable emotional state.

In specific situations

The anger troubles we have can be attributed to the events or situations we have encountered, both in the past and present. If an individual is raised during childhood in an environment characterized by a regular exposure to feelings of threat and injustice, it has the potential to cultivate a latent sense of rage inside them. However, as individuals mature, they persist in harboring this resentment, and any circumstance that appears to pose a risk contributes to the accumulation of wrath. Individuals often develop a cognitive predisposition to perceive situations as threatening or unjust, even when objective evidence suggests otherwise. Consequently, such individuals tend to respond to these situations with feelings of anger and subsequently engage in corresponding behavioral responses. Moreover, when confronted with a multitude of difficulties and challenges, individuals may experience a sense of being overwhelmed, leading to a heightened emotional response characterized by anger directed towards both relevant and irrelevant factors.

There exist various variables that contribute to the experience of anger in human beings. Due to individual differences in coping mechanisms, certain individuals possess the ability to effectively regulate their anger, while others may struggle in this regard. If an individual lacks the ability to effectively manage their anger, it serves as evidence of the presence of anger-related difficulties. In the subsequent sub-chapter, we will delve into the topic of identifying the presence of rage disorders.

Recognizing and Assessing Anger-related Challenges

Numerous individuals in society exhibit anger-related difficulties, often lacking awareness of the problematic nature of their anger. There is a prevalent belief among individuals that experiencing anger, displaying outbursts, and even engaging in acts of violence are considered to be within the realm of normal behavior. There are individuals who hold the belief that their capacity to suppress their anger implies the absence of an anger-related problem. However, the reality remains that regardless of whether one believes they are justified in expressing anger and having outbursts, or if they perceive themselves as composed by suppressing their anger, it is evident that they possess unresolved anger problems. There exists a prevailing belief among individuals that aggression is indicative of anger-related symptoms; however, it is important to acknowledge that aggression can manifest independently of anger difficulties.

Individuals who struggle with regulating their anger or exhibit excessive anger beyond what is deemed appropriate in emotional contexts are frequently diagnosed with various forms of anger disorders. Various forms of anger disorders exist, each characterized by distinct indicators and symptoms that facilitate their identification. The following are two anger disorders that are widely recognized and commonly identifiable, along with their respective symptoms:

The concept of passive anger refers to a form of anger expression that is characterized by indirect or subtle behaviors rather than overt or direct confrontation

The majority of individuals who encounter passive anger often remain unaware of their emotional state of fury. Passive rage is characterized as a form of fury that is not shown through physical means. This phenomenon may also be denoted as tacit anger. Passive rage refers to those who suppress or restrain their feelings of anger, choosing not to express or release these emotions outwardly. Individuals who experience quiet anger may not consistently exhibit overt signs of wrath. In reality, individuals often lack awareness of their shown emotion, which is frequently identified as rage. Conversely, individuals may conceal their true emotions by expressing them through other affective states, such as hostility, irony, inflexibility, delay, animosity, withdrawal, or even indifference. Passive anger may not invariably manifest as physical aggression, and those harboring passive anger may not necessarily engage in behaviors that directly impact the individuals who provoked their anger. Conversely, individuals engage in behaviors that primarily impact their own well-being, such as truancy or absenteeism from educational or occupational settings, social withdrawal from their social networks, deliberate avoidance of interpersonal interactions, deliberate underperformance in academic or professional domains, or even turning to the consumption of illicit substances. From the perspective of those in their social circle, it may appear that these individuals are deliberately isolating themselves or engaging in self-destructive behaviors. However, it is important to acknowledge that often these individuals themselves are unaware of their own actions and motivations. The inherent nature of passive anger being consistently suppressed poses challenges in its identification and recognition. However, seeking assistance can significantly contribute to the exploration of the underlying emotions or causes of anger, as well as the development of effective coping strategies. Suppressing one's anger is not beneficial for oneself or for others in the immediate vicinity. In reality, individuals are subjecting themselves to more harm.

Determine the Stimuli That Elicit Anger

Understanding the factors that elicit anger might facilitate the management of this emotional state. Various factors can elicit anger in individuals, and these triggers vary due to the inherent diversity among individuals. Nevertheless, other prevalent instances of mistreatment are commonly encountered by individuals, including but not limited to, instances of inequitable or unjust conduct, instances of being undermined, instances of being belittled, instances of being subjected to embarrassment, and instances of physical intimidation. Triggers may encompass various factors, such as experiencing sorrow, encountering financial concerns, enduring excessive stress, and being employed in a high-pressure occupation.

The task at hand involves the identification of signals.

This inquiry pertains to the identification of several physiological and behavioral indicators, including sensations of irritation, the onset of annoyance, perspiration, facial flushing, and the act of clenching one's jaw or fists. Individuals may potentially encounter physiological responses such as an increased heart rate or the onset of a headache. In certain cases, individuals may even perceive visual disturbances, such as the perception of dots, which may serve as an indication to remove oneself from the present surroundings.

Exploring Alternative Methods for Channeling Anger in a Healthier Manner

In order to effectively manage and channel feelings of anger, it is advisable to seek alternative methods of expression that do not result in detrimental consequences to one's physical and emotional well-being. It is advisable to keep objects such as stress balls or bean bags readily accessible in close proximity, as they can serve as alternative outlets for physical tension release, hence mitigating the need to resort to using one's fists. Managing anger can be challenging, although rather than reacting impulsively, it can be beneficial to temporarily disengage and employ anger management strategies to mitigate the escalating feelings of rage.

Exploring Strategies to Manage Anger

Individuals who possess the ability to recognize their triggers and perceive the initial signs of anger are more adept at effectively managing and preemptively addressing their rage. Explore several strategies and experiment with their efficacy in mitigating the intensifying fury within oneself. It is possible to observe that a particular technique may yield favorable results in a specific context, while proving ineffective in a different scenario. Adopting a different cognitive framework is a strategic approach that yields optimal outcomes over an extended period, facilitating the transformation of pessimistic cognitions into more optimistic ones.

Reconsidering Perspectives On Life

Challenges are an inherent aspect of human existence. Regardless of the extent of one's efforts to cultivate proficient strategies for managing challenging circumstances or the level of determination to maintain composure in the midst of adversity, it is inevitable that life will persist in presenting novel and unforeseen obstacles. Instances of adversity can manifest in several forms, such as unemployment, illness, marital discord, the imprudent actions of others, targeted gossip, unjust treatment in professional or educational settings, and similar circumstances. Therefore, it is imperative to cultivate a realistic mindset when contemplating tragedy, perceiving it as a disagreeable inconvenience. The vast majority of stimuli that incite anger, irrespective of their perceived severity in the immediate context, typically result in minimal consequences such as wasted time, compromised self-respect, or financial loss. These circumstances possess a social dimension. Nonetheless, these occurrences do not pose a significant risk to one's life, which is why they are commonly referred to as inconveniences.

This chapter provides an introduction to six irrational cognitive tendencies and proposes six alternative strategies for cultivating a more rational and intelligent mindset when faced with challenges and adversity, with the aim of reducing anger. The approach that will be taught is straightforward in nature, however it may provide challenges in its execution. To foster a novel perspective on the challenging facets of one's life, it is vital to cultivate cognizance of irrational thinking and dedicate time to honing the skill of employing alternative concepts. The objective is to induce a change in one's perspective towards the world, resulting in a reduced emotional response to daily challenges and inconveniences.

Similar to all individuals, you possess the capacity for cognitive thought. In essence, individuals are consistently engaged in the process of perceiving, observing, interpreting, assessing, and forming judgments regarding occurrences within their lives, rather than merely responding to them. The cognitive perspective posits that an individual's thought processes significantly impact their emotional experiences and subsequent behavioral responses. One's cognitive processes have a significant role in the experience of rage and the subsequent engagement in self-defeating behaviors associated with anger. Over the course of time, individuals, including oneself, have inevitably acquired cognitive patterns, which have become ingrained and rigid due to years of consistent repetition.

Similar to the majority of individuals, it is likely that you are unaware of the cognitive processes that occur when confronted with a stimulus that elicits anger. Indeed, the cognitive processes and resultant thoughts that one experiences may appear to be entirely ordinary and acceptable due to the prolonged utilization of these patterns and ideations over an extensive period of time. Developing a heightened understanding of one's cognitive processes during episodes of anger, and subsequently modifying deeply ingrained thought patterns, play a pivotal role in mitigating anger levels. It is imperative to invest diligent effort and engage in deliberate practice in order to alter one's cognitive perspective on unpleasant occurrences. However, it is encouraging to note that such exertion and practice will effectively diminish feelings of rage while concurrently augmenting sensations of joy and contentment. Do you hold the belief that external individuals are responsible for eliciting rage within you through their disagreeable and undesirable actions? If such is indeed the case, you are committing the error that was previously discussed in chapter 2, which we referred to as the significant mistake.

However, it is important to acknowledge that individuals possess the ability to govern their thought processes, so exerting a greater degree of influence over their anger than they may initially perceive.

For instance, consider a scenario where one finds themselves navigating a heavily trafficked expressway, when an adjacent motorist abruptly veers into their designated lane of travel. Upon applying the brakes and emitting a cautionary honk, the individual in question responded with an angry honk and a gesture involving the extension of the middle finger. It is evident that individuals may exhibit a variety of responses to this particular situation. Could any of the following eight thoughts perhaps result in a diminished or negligible experience of anger?

The individual in question exhibits behavior that is deemed inappropriate and warrants a need for corrective action.

I possess no knowledge regarding the individual in question. It is possible that he was not attentive. I will refrain from pursuing the matter further.

Whom does he perceive himself to be? I am unwilling to tolerate this substandard quality. I will demonstrate to him that I am not experiencing feelings of intimidation.

I find myself becoming less inclined to respond to such matters due to the advancing years. I possess the ability to maintain a state of composure and assertiveness.

The individual's behavior is deemed inappropriate. The individual in question is exhibiting a significant degree of unfairness, given it is they who failed to allocate their attention appropriately.

It would be desirable if all drivers exhibited equitable and thoughtful behavior; nevertheless, a subset of drivers deviate from this expectation.

This is a reflection of the current state of affairs in the world.

The actions he is engaging in are quite objectionable. I am unwilling to tolerate it.

This is not a significant matter. There is no obligation on me to respond.

It is evident that thoughts 2, 4, 6, and 8 are more inclined to result in minimal rage.

What are the cognitive processes involved in the development of adaptive strategies for anger management? Cognitive behavioral therapists, such as Albert Ellis and Aaron Beck, have made significant contributions to the advancement of a four-step process aimed at facilitating the reassessment and modification of cognitive patterns.

Methods for Identifying Triggers

Identifying triggers can be a challenging endeavor. Occasionally, stimuli can be quite inconspicuous, to the extent that their presence may go unnoticed.

However, it is important to acknowledge that triggers do exist. So, it is vital for you to keep an eye out for the unmistakable warning signals that you've been triggered.

Here is a list of red flags I've noticed during my career as a mother and educator.

A trigger has gotten to you when you feel you can't get a grasp on your reaction or feelings.

A trigger has gotten to you when you feel profoundly hurt by anything your child has said or done.

When you overreact or blow a situation out of proportion, a trigger has gotten to you.

When you lose your temper instantly, seemingly for no reason, a trigger has gotten to you.

A trigger has gotten to you when you feel like you've gone through this before but somehow feel powerless to modify your reactions.

A trigger has gotten to you when you are shrieking, sweating, and busting veins from your forehead.

When you realize you desire to physically damage your child, such as grabbing them by the arm or spanking them, a trigger has gotten to you.

In particular, the last red flag is of major concern. If you ever feel the need to use physical force to "discipline" your child, it is a clear warning that you need to gain a hold on your emotions and behaviors. Violence is never the answer. As a result, whenever you feel like using physical force on your child, you must quickly move away and cool down. It is always best to confront the matter once you have cooled down.

Please remember that identifying rage as soon as possible assists you to keep your emotions in check. Consequently, you greatly boost your odds of staying cool even a highly irritating scenario.

Beyond parenting triggers that originate from your child's conduct, other triggers emerge from our background.

How so?

In his book Parenting from the Inside Out: How a greater self-understanding can help you raise children who flourish, Dan Siegel explores how parents perceive their children from the perspective of how they were parented. In other words, we tend to react like our parents did. For example, persons who grew up in an abusive environment may feel obliged to replicate the same habits. These patterns are so delicate that they are nearly undetectable to the individual. They are apparent as day to others but not to the individual.

Based on Dr. Siegel's theory, we must take the time to learn how our parents treated us. We must deconstruct how our parents got it right and how they got it wrong. From there, we may assess patterns that we need to change. Specifically, we can determine why our reactions may occasionally become out of hand.

Of course, not everyone comes from a problematic home. Persons from loving households tend to reproduce the same patterns with their children. People that grow up with loving and supporting parents often employ the same parenting method with their children.

Now, if you didn't have loving and supporting parents, does that imply you're condemned to repeat the same patterns?

Of course not!

You see, we all have a choice. We can choose to sustain unhealthy or even harmful patterns with our kids. Conversely, we can choose to break habits that negatively affect us growing up.

This choice is yours.

If you were fortunate to have loving and supportive parents, I would encourage you to look through your upbringing and assess how your parents got it right. From there, you can integrate those beneficial patterns into your parenting approach.

Ultimately, we have the capacity to transform our world right now! That shift begins with a conscious choice to improve our children's lives more than ours. I know that's what you want for your kids. Otherwise, we wouldn't be having this discussion right now.

Addressing Triggers at an Early Stage

After conducting a thorough examination of triggers, it is imperative to address strategies for effectively mitigating their impact. Our objective is to prevent them from exerting influence over us any longer. Our objective is to consistently maintain control and authority over the situation. Therefore, I have compiled a comprehensive reference section that will empower you to effectively manage positive triggers.

This section provides useful tips and strategies for effectively managing triggers in a comprehensive manner. I can guarantee that upon completion of this part, your perception of rage will undergo a transformative shift.

The concept of the Anger Iceberg

Anger, similar to an iceberg, possesses hidden depths beyond what is readily apparent. The observable segment of an iceberg constitutes merely 10% of its overall bulk. Likewise, the outward manifestation of fury represents only a fraction of its underlying depth. Indeed, fury can be regarded as the ultimate outcome resulting from various underlying factors.

A comprehensive examination of the "anger iceberg" phenomena was conducted in a 2020 study, with a particular focus on its implications within the field of counselling. This study highlights the notion that rage is not an isolated occurrence. On the contrary, rage can be understood as a resultant emotional response to many stressors that are present in the individual's environment. This intriguing investigation specifically examined the prevalence of burnout as a contributing factor to the development of anger-related problems. The outcomes of the study indicate that burnout serves as a reliable indicator for the presence of anger management difficulties. The numerical value provided by the user is.

Postpone The Manifestation Of Emotional Anger.

Excessive verbal expression at a state of intense anger can yield unfavourable consequences.

The term that inflicts the most profound emotional pain is the term that remains unuttered.

Allow the counterpart to engage in a dispute until the turbulent situation has subsided, subsequently prompting them to engage in introspection over the unexpressed thoughts and ideas.

James Whitcomb Riley was an American poet, writer, and journalist. He was born on October 7, 1849, in Greenfield, Indiana, and passed

This can alternatively be construed as engaging in self-imposed isolation.

Timeout involves disengaging from a situation of heightened anger, ceasing an ongoing dispute, engaging in deep breathing exercises, and employing any other strategies that may aid in achieving a state of calmness, as opposed to responding vehemently to the provoking stimulus.

The act of taking a timeout is a cultivated behaviour that should be regularly implemented. The act of contemplating allows individuals to arrive at more informed decisions.

In a situation that elicits anger, the cognitive process may be impeded due to the involvement of intense emotions. However, the implementation of a time out allows individuals to temporarily disengage from the situation, facilitating an opportunity to reflect upon and analyse the circumstances from various vantage points.

Postponing the expression of rage allows for introspection over the appropriateness and validity of one's emotional response to the given circumstances.

Additionally, it provides the capability to perform the following actions:

Please identify the precise issue that led to the emergence of conflict.

The decision to address or overlook a conflict can be determined by evaluating the necessity of raising the issue.

It is imperative to cultivate a mindset that promotes rational and pragmatic deliberation regarding both personal and collective rights. In doing so, one must conscientiously determine appropriate courses of action, verbal expressions, and equitable resolutions that uphold the interests and well-being of all involved parties.

Initially, a number of observable manifestations of rage can be identified. Indications of anger or an impending outburst may manifest in one's physiological state. Several examples will comprise:

The sensation of dizziness.

2. The presence of tremor or tremors occurring in various regions of the body.

3. Sensation of facial and cervical warmth accompanying the physiological phenomenon of increased blood flow.

Sweetness can be detected not just on the palms but also in other regions.

A phenomenon characterised by the initiation and subsequent intensification of heart rate beyond its typical range.

The individual is experiencing symptoms of abdominal discomfort and cranial discomfort.

7. Perform oral hygiene practises such as cleaning the jaw or grinding the teeth.

Another issue that individuals may observe when experiencing the onset of rage is a shift in their emotional state. The proliferation of emotions is anticipated to occur ubiquitously, and their responses may deviate from anticipated norms. There are various emotional states that an individual experiencing anger may undergo.

One may have the inclination to engage in aggressive behaviour towards another individual. The nature of this phenomenon may manifest either through spoken or bodily means.

The individual may experience feelings of anxiety and resentment towards the other party.

Frequently, individuals experience feelings of guilt when confronted with anger due to their aversion to such emotional states and their desire for emotional dissipation.

It is possible that individuals may experience emotions characterised by depression and sadness.

Numerous individuals express their discontent over their emotional state of anger, discussing their feelings of irritation towards a specific individual and a particular circumstance.

It is frequently seen that individuals may experience a desire to seek relief from their current circumstances.

Individuals who are confronted with persistent rage are prone to encountering the aforementioned consequences, often without being cognizant of their occurrence. There may exist a component within oneself that proves challenging to discern from one's typical emotions and actions. This observation may be indicative of a negative indication, although it remains challenging to ascertain the presence of an anger-related issue.

If one is seeking to ascertain the nature of their anger and determine the necessity of employing the tactics outlined in this guide, several observable cues such as gestures, voice variations, and other related factors might be attended to. One may identify the impending onset of anger by observing the following indicators. Should these manifestations occur with regularity, it is advisable to seek assistance in managing anger and restoring one's overall well-being. Additional indicators and manifestations of violence that one could see encompass:

The individual exhibits emotional distress by engaging in behaviours such as crying, screaming, or yelling within the context of a discussion or conversation.

In interpersonal communication, individuals may employ an elevated vocal tone, often surpassing the necessary level, with the intention of inducing fear or intimidation in the recipient.

The individual experiences certain urges. The following items are typically considered to be detrimental to one's health, however they possess the potential to induce a state of relaxation. This implies a desire for activities such as smoking, drinking, or engaging with comparable substances.

The individual begins to exhibit behaviour that is characterised by being confrontational or displaying abusive tendencies.

One experiences a loss of one's sense of humour, resulting in a lack of amusement or comedic appreciation.

The frequent utilisation of sarcasm becomes a common practise.

The act of ambulation is initiated. This phenomenon might occur in the presence of others or in solitude.

To simulate a confrontational stance, position one hand into a closed fist while maintaining a poised demeanour, suggesting preparedness to engage in physical altercation with the other individual.

The act of rubbing one's head

The ability to identify these indicators is of utmost significance in facilitating the management of one's anger. It is not uncommon for individuals to become engrossed in their personal sphere and disregard the potential impact of their pursuits on both their own well-being and the well-being of others. However, it is imperative to acknowledge that harbouring anger will invariably exert an influence on both oneself and the individuals in one's immediate vicinity. Developing the ability to regulate one's emotions and assuming personal responsibility for them can contribute to the enhancement of physical, mental, and emotional well-being, as well as facilitate the restoration of interpersonal connections.

Now, it is necessary to allocate a brief period of time to direct our attention towards the process of discerning the various stimuli that appear to elicit feelings of rage inside oneself. Every individual possesses at least one stimulus that tends to elicit their fervour, whether it is a distinct circumstance, a specific individual, or another factor. When individuals are in close proximity to this stimulus, they exhibit heightened vigilance and preparedness for a confrontation, in anticipation of an impending event. Understanding the specific stimuli that elicit our anger and implementing strategies to minimise exposure to these triggers can significantly enhance our ability to effectively manage our anger.

Numerous prevalent stimuli exist that individuals commonly encounter, which exacerbate the issue of rage beyond its initial magnitude. Several commonly seen passion triggers that might be emphasised are:

Experiencing inequitable treatment

The experience of being mistreated is generally disliked by individuals. When individuals see an unjust event, it is common for them to experience a range of negative emotions, such as irritation, distress, and occasionally anger.

Regrettably, instances of inequitable occurrences are inevitable for individuals irrespective of their affiliations or diligent efforts, and such incidents can manifest with notable frequency. Several instances of this can be observed, such as:

In the given scenario, an individual finds themselves in a queue, awaiting access to a particular destination, while another individual procceds to bypass them and position themselves ahead in the queue.

In the academic context, a scenario may arise where a teacher evaluates an examination or assignment and assigns a grade that the student perceives as not commensurate with their anticipated level of achievement.

The individual responsible for assessing your performance in the workplace is your supervisor, and you see their appraisal to lack precision.

The individual in question receives a citation from a law enforcement official, despite their firm belief that they were not exceeding the speed limit at the given moment.

Managing certain injustices in life can be challenging; nonetheless, it is essential to acknowledge that such occurrences are inherent to the nature of life. The nature of existence is such that fairness is not guaranteed, and circumstances may not always align with one's desires. The ability to exert control over the aforementioned situation is limited, and any attempts to do so may exacerbate the circumstances. However, one does possess agency in determining their response to the perceived injustice. Individuals have the option to respond in a composed and constructive manner, so effectively resolving the situation, or they may opt to react with rage, leading to illogical behaviour and exacerbating the situation.

Theory Of Interactionism

The theoretical framework known as the labelling theory, as well as the concept of deviance introduced by Becker (1973), provide a valuable understanding of the processes involved in categorising an action as deviant and subsequently labelling the individual who performs said action as "deviant." The hypothesis posits that all deviant behaviour is a consequence of societal factors. In this context, it might be argued that no action or person is inherently deviant, but rather acquires deviant status through social processes that involve a response from society. These processes encompass the formation of norms and social regulations that are expected to be adhered to by all members of a given social collective, hence delineating behaviours that are deemed as morally acceptable or unacceptable. Deviance is a term used to characterise any violation of established norms and social regulations, resulting in the labelling of the transgressor as a "deviant" individual. Multiple conceptualizations of deviance have been put forth, encompassing (1) a statistical approach that characterises deviance as the departure from the average or norm, and (2) a medical framework that views deviance as a manifestation of illness or pathology. (3) Certain sociologists conceptualise it by employing the framework of functionality and dysfunctionality, wherein dysfunctional behaviours are indicative of social disorganisation. Additionally, (4) alternative sociological perspectives define it as the lack of adherence to established norms within a specific social collective (Becker, 1973). According to Becker (1973), those who continue to employ these definitions of deviance fail to acknowledge the intricate nature of the process involved in defining deviant behaviour, especially in relation to situations that are characterised by ambiguity. Furthermore, the aforementioned definitions primarily rely on the deviant act committed, whereas Becker (1973) presents a different perspective on deviance. According to Becker, deviance is not solely defined by the act itself, but rather emerges from the social interaction in which a collective assigns the label of "deviant" to an individual who is believed to have violated societal norms.

The process of labelling plays a crucial role in the formation of deviance. According to Becker (1973), an act may be theoretically classified as a violation of social norms and regulations. However, it is only when this conduct elicits a social response inside the public arena that it is deemed deviant and the individual responsible for the act is labelled as such. In his seminal work, Becker (1973) provides an illustrative case of incest, wherein the classification of deviance is contingent upon the presence of public allegations against the perpetrator, despite the act being deemed a violation of societal norms and regulations within specific social circles. In contrast, in cases where incestuous behaviour elicits only a limited response, such as informal discussions or rumours, without resulting in formal public allegations, it may not be universally seen as a deviant behaviour. On the other hand, an individual may be categorised as deviant despite their lack of violation of established norms or social regulations, only due to the perception that the social response to their behaviour is deemed troublesome. Consider the scenario of an individual who engages in the act of exchanging phone texts during a conference, all the while their device's ring volume is set to its maximum level. While there may not be a formal prohibition on the use of telephones during the conference, engaging in such behaviour could elicit a negative response from other attendees who regard it as disruptive or inappropriate. These instances illustrate the significant variability in the reactions to a particular "deviant" behaviour.

According to Becker's (1973) findings, the social response exhibits temporal variation, contingent upon the characteristics of the individual who perpetrates and experiences the act, as well as the nature of the resulting consequences. Certain deviations manifest at specific intervals, while others gradually dissipate over a period of time. In the past, homosexuality was widely regarded as a deviant behaviour or mental health disorder (Spector and Kitsuse, 2001). However, a significant shift occurred in 1973 when it was no longer classified as such in the Diagnostic and Statistical Manual of Mental Disorders. Consequently, attitudes towards homosexuality have evolved, and contemporary society generally exhibits reduced negative social reactions towards it, if any. Certain individuals are disproportionately subjected to the "deviant" label compared to others, specifically those who belong to marginalised groups, have a criminalised status, or possess a lower social class, even when engaging in identical behaviours and adhering to the same social norms and regulations. In a similar vein, an act of deviance perpetrated against an individual or a collective with a prominent social standing or identifiable attributes (such as race, socioeconomic class, occupation, and so forth) assumes greater societal significance and is more prone to elicit a negative social response, particularly when directed towards an individual of lower social standing. The social reaction elicited will also be contingent upon the repercussions of the aberrant behaviour. In his seminal work, Becker (1973) provides an illustrative case study involving adolescent females who participate in unauthorised sexual behaviour. These acts may not necessarily lead to condemnation or societal disapproval, in and of themselves. In the event that such actions lead to a pregnancy, the individuals involved, particularly the female party, are prone to experiencing disapproval or societal condemnation.

Tips For Maintaining Healthy Relationships And Managing Anger

Ideally, it is expected that all individuals involved in a relationship should assume complete accountability for their respective behaviours. The aforementioned assertion does not hold true universally, and indeed, the undesirable consequence under discussion pertains to the emotional state of anger, with feelings of annoyance, disgust, and negativity.

Both parties involved must engage in a candid and forthright exchange regarding the underlying causes of their anger. The crux of the issue often lies in the manner in which this anger is expressed, which typically gives rise to complications.

This can be a challenging task in certain occasions. It is imperative to establish a clear differentiation between the act of expressing anger and serving as a manifestation or consequence of one's anger. The concept may initially appear paradoxical; nevertheless, upon further consideration, comprehension can be achieved.

The presence of concealed stimuli may not always be readily apparent to individuals experiencing anger. It is imperative for individuals to possess an awareness of these emotions and demonstrate a willingness to articulate them, rather than suppressing or disregarding them.

5. Demonstrate qualities of love, care, and affection.

One aspect that is occasionally disregarded is the manner in which we communicate with others. It is important to effectively communicate a sense of affection through the modulation of one's voice and the selection of appropriate vocabulary. Distinguish between the commercial colleague and a personal relationship partner. One should strive to refrain from engaging in what Drs. John and Julie Gottman have termed as the "Four Horsemen of the Apocalypse."

Criticism is an evaluative process wherein individuals express their disapproval or dissatisfaction with a particular

Contempt, defensiveness, and stonewalling are three negative communication behaviours that can hinder effective interpersonal interactions. According to Gottman's research, several behaviours have been found to be indicative of early divorce, often occurring approximately 5.6 years following the marriage ceremony. The study revealed that emotional disengagement and anger were significant predictors of divorce, occurring on average 16.2 years following the marriage ceremony. Gottman's research emphasises the significance of maintaining a positive-to-negative ratio of 0.8 or lower in one's interpersonal exchanges with their romantic partner. The concept involves consistently allocating resources towards the "emotional bank account" of a relationship by active participation in compassionate and affectionate actions. When an individual's emotional bank account is replete with pleasant interactions, there is a higher likelihood of attributing negative interactions to factors such as their spouse experiencing a challenging day or being preoccupied, rather than ascribing them to their partner possessing unfavourable qualities.

Demonstrate composure.

One effective approach to imparting constructive anger management skills to youngsters is through the demonstration of appropriate behaviour by adults. Utilise these challenging instances as opportunities to impart immediate lessons to your child on the art of relaxation.For illustrative purposes, let us take the following example: Suppose an individual receives a telephone call from an automotive repair facility, wherein they are informed that the initial cost estimate for their vehicle has now increased double. You are experiencing intense anger, while your youngster is in close proximity, observing your behaviour attentively. Utilise your reservoir of composure to provide an immediate lesson in anger management for your youngster. "I am currently experiencing a strong feeling of anger," you calmly communicate to your youngster. The cost of repairing my car was increased double by the mechanic. Subsequently, a calming resolution can be proposed: "I intend to engage in a brisk walk in order to restore my energy levels." Children tend to emulate the behaviour of their parents.

Cease your current activity and inhale deeply.

One of the most formidable aspects of parenting is when our children articulate their anger towards us. If one fails to exercise caution, the tantrums exhibited by individuals can incite hitherto unknown emotions inside oneself. It is important to exercise caution as the emotion of wrath has the potential to spread and influence others. It is advisable to establish an initial rule within one's household, stating: "Within this dwelling, we endeavour to address challenges in a composed and authoritative manner." The law can subsequently be consistently strengthened.Here is an illustrative instance of how one could effectively implement the aforementioned concept. In situations where a kid is experiencing distress and requires prompt resolution, it may be appropriate to communicate the need for a temporary pause. Let us defer this discussion to a later time. Subsequently, depart in a calm manner without providing a response. According to a maternal informant, her sole means of escape involved secluding herself within the confines of the lavatory. The male child persisted in engaging in repetitive kicking and vocalising in a high-pitched manner, while the female individual maintained her position of not emerging from her current location until such time as the male child exhibited a state of emotional tranquilly. The toddler required several instances of confinement to comprehend the seriousness of the situation. Subsequently, the boy acquired the understanding that his mother would solely engage in conversations regarding the matter when he exhibited composure and assertiveness.

Construct a lexicon encompassing a range of affective states.

Numerous children exhibit tantrum behaviours due to their limited ability to effectively communicate their dissatisfaction through alternative means. Engaging in physical actions such as kicking, yelling, cursing, punching, or hurling items may represent the limited repertoire of expressive means available to them. Inquiring about the child's emotional state by asking, "Please articulate your feelings," may prove impractical as they might not have acquired the necessary skills to effectively express their emotions. Collaboratively create a visual representation of affective vocabulary by means of a feeling word poster. Initiate the process by proposing the following prompt: "Let us collectively generate an extensive array of lexemes that can effectively convey our intense anger towards another individual." Subsequently, compile and display the participants' suggested terms on the poster.Angry, angry, furious, irritated, ticked off, and enraged represent a limited selection of examples. One should generate a cartographic representation of the aforementioned entities, display it in a prominent location, and engage in consistent utilisation of said entities. When a child experiences distress, it is recommended to employ the following vocabulary in order to facilitate their practical application: "It appears that you are exhibiting signs of intense anger." Would you like to engage in a discussion regarding the matter at hand?" in addition to "Your demeanour appears to indicate a high level of irritation." Is engaging in physical activity through walking sufficient for you to alleviate the issue? Subsequently, throughout the course of the day, it is advisable to continuously augment the compilation of emotional descriptors by incorporating newly encountered terms that arise during opportune instances conducive to learning.

Design a promotional poster aimed at fostering a state of relaxation.

There exists a wide array of techniques aimed at assisting children in achieving a state of calmness when they initially experience agitation. Regrettably, a number of children have been deprived of the chance to contemplate alternative possibilities. Consequently, individuals find themselves encountering difficulties as they possess limited knowledge regarding appropriate means of expressing their frustration, thereby resorting to unacceptable behaviours. Therefore, it is advisable to engage in activities that promote the development of more suitable replacement behaviours with your child. One possible approach would be to create a sizable poster displaying a comprehensive enumeration of the aforementioned items. The following recommendations are provided: One potential approach to managing stress and finding solace is to engage in a variety of activities. These activities may include physically distancing oneself from the source of stress, mentally picturing a serene environment, engaging in physical exercise, listening to music, venting frustration by striking a pillow, participating in sports such as basketball, expressing oneself through art, seeking social interaction by conversing with others, or engaging in vocal expression through singing. After the child has chosen their preferred "calm down" strategy, it is advisable to provide them with ongoing encouragement to utilise it whenever they experience emotional distress.

Develop an understanding of the initial indicators.

It is important to communicate to one's child that individuals commonly exhibit subtle indicators that signal an imminent emotional outburst. It is vital to allocate our focus towards them, since they possess the capacity to prevent us from encountering adverse circumstances. Subsequently, instructing one's offspring to discern conspicuous indicators that imply the onset of agitation is advisable.For instance, the individual exhibits heightened vocal volume, facial redness, hand tension, increased heart rate, oral dehydration, and accelerated respiration. Once individuals become conscious of these factors, it is advisable to draw their attention to them in the event that they experience annoyance. It appears that you are experiencing a loss of control. Additionally, the hands have formed a clinched fist. Do you get feelings of intense anger?" The cultivation of children's awareness of early indicators of anger and irritation can contribute to their ability to self-regulate and achieve a state of calmness. Additionally, this period presents an opportune moment to employ strategies for anger management. The intensity of anger tends to increase rapidly, and delaying intervention until a kid reaches a state of extreme emotional distress is typically ineffective in restoring control.

Instruct individuals on anger management strategies and methodologies.

The utilisation of the "3 + 10" strategy has been found to be efficacious in promoting emotional regulation among children. One such approach could involve reproducing the formula on oversized sheets of paper and strategically displaying them about one's residence. Next, provide the child with clear instructions on how to effectively implement the given formula. It is advisable to promptly do two actions upon perceiving any indications from one's body that control is being compromised. Begin by inhaling deeply and slowly, allowing your breath to originate from your abdominal region. Repeat this process three times. Illustrate this concept to your child. Demonstrate the technique of deep breathing to individuals, followed by providing instructions to mentally envision themselves situated on an escalator. Commence the ascent from the lowest step and proceed gradually on the escalator while utilising this opportunity to rest. Continue persevering! Descend the escalator in a deliberate manner, exhaling in a leisurely and controlled manner simultaneously. This brings us to a total of three. Please engage in a deliberate and measured mental process of sequentially enumerating from one to ten. This results in a cumulative sum of ten. When the numerical values of 3 and 10 are combined, the resulting sum has a calming effect on an individual.

A straightforward approach to elucidate the profound influence of our breath is to draw a parallel between its functionality and that of a remote control, which governs the operations of our body and brain. When a youngster experiences distress or annoyance, their sympathetic nervous system becomes activated, resulting in rapid and shallow breathing. The practise of deep breathing has been found to enhance the functionality of the vagus nerve in children, hence stimulating the parasympathetic nervous system and facilitating the process of relaxation and regulation of emotions such as anger and anxiety. Engaging in deep breathing exercises is considered to be a simple and effective method for children to achieve a state of relaxation.

It has been observed that equipping children with three preferred breathing strategies empowers them while preventing exhaustion for both the children and the adults involved.There exist numerous inventive and tangible strategies to foster creativity and concreteness in the practise of deep breathing for a child experiencing anger. However, I will present a selection of my preferred techniques:

The act of extinguishing birthday candles. Extend all ten digits of the hand and instruct them to exhale in a deliberate and unhurried manner, aiming to extinguish the candles at a leisurely pace.

It is important to maintain a steady breathing pattern while executing a hand-drawing technique. Maintain a raised hand position, inhaling while tracing a vertical trajectory upwards, and exhaling gradually while descending along the finger.

The subject of discussion is Elsa. The act of respiration. Engage in a deliberate inhalation through your nasal passage, ensuring the deepest and most extensive intake of breath possible, followed by a gradual exhalation through your oral cavity, with the intention of creating an extraordinary ice sculpture.

The practise of Rainbow Breathing. Commence the inhalation process from the lowermost point of the crimson arch, while ascending the spectrum of colours represented by the rainbow. Subsequently, exhale while descending, with the option to incorporate an arbitrary number of additional hues.

The practise of dandelion breathing. Inhale the scent emitted by the dandelion and thereafter exhale at a controlled pace through the oral cavity, therefore dispersing the seeds and engaging in the act of expressing a wish.

The practise of Figure 8 breathing. Perform a motion resembling the shape of the numeral "eight" either in the atmosphere or on a solid plane, while inhaling during one half of the motion and exhaling during the other half, with a brief pause at the midpoint.

Teaching youngsters a novel approach to managing their anger in a healthy manner can be a formidable task, especially when they have predominantly relied on aggressive coping mechanisms. The acquisition of new habits takes a minimum of 21 consecutive days of consistent repetition. I would like to propose the following suggestion: Select a singular approach that is deemed essential for your child's achievement and allocate a few minutes each day, for a minimum duration of 21 days, to concentrate on it. The probability of your youngster acquiring the new skill is further enhanced due to their consistent practise of the same approach, as this is a fundamental aspect of skill acquisition. Moreover, it is the most efficacious method to impede the proliferation of violence and facilitate the cultivation of a more prosperous and harmonious existence for one's offspring.

Certain approaches may exhibit greater efficacy than others when considering the well-being of your infant. Furthermore, it should be noted that interventions that have proven effective for one child or parent may not always yield the same results for an individual in a different context. Moreover, it should be noted that the efficacy of tactics employed to manage a tantrum in the past may not necessarily translate to future situations. When a kid is experiencing a tantrum, it is imperative to prioritise their safety and ensure that they are not at risk of causing injury to themselves or others. During an episode of emotional

dysregulation, children frequently experience a loss of bodily control.

If an individual is situated within their residence, it may be advisable to relocate them to a more tranquil setting, such as their bedroom. Conversely, if they are situated outside the home, it would be preferable to shift them to a secluded area with less pedestrian activity. Next, consider the potential negative outcomes that could occur. Exclude hunger, nappy changes, and fatigue as potential factors. The observed behaviour could perhaps be attributed to behavioural crying, or it may indicate a desire for physical contact and attention. It is possible that the individuals in question may be experiencing either insufficient or excessive levels of stimulation. It is possible that they desire to venture outdoors, a course of action that could yield advantageous outcomes. The individual in question may be experiencing symptoms indicative of gastrointestinal gas or colic. It is advisable to focus on the process of reducing the number of available choices. Engaging in this task can be perceived as laborious and lacking in appreciation.Allocate a portion of your schedule for personal self-care and introspection. Engage in a tranquil bathing experience. After ensuring the well-being of your child, the following strategies might be employed to address a tantrum exhibited by a toddler:

Disregard the occurrence and promote the completion of your child's tantrum. Navigating around public spaces or operating a vehicle can provide difficulties. If one is operating a motor vehicle, it is advisable to exercise patience and wait, if feasible, until the tantrum has subsided. When in a public setting, it is important to acknowledge that tantrums are a normal occurrence and that permitting children to express their emotions is beneficial for their well-being in that moment.

Utilise a literary or plaything item to redirect the focus of your child. Optimal results can be achieved by redirecting the child's focus immediately before to the onset of a tantrum. This approach may prove ineffective in the event that the individual is exhibiting a comprehensive display of tantrum behaviour. If the child in question is over the age of two, it is recommended to either alter their physical location or place them in a designated period of silent reflection. Removing external stimuli might also contribute to promoting relaxation in your youngster.

Retain custody of your child till he or she regains emotional composure. Depending on the characteristics of the tantrum, it may be more effective to adopt a seated position on the floor and encircle one's arms about the body. There is no chance of dropping them in the event that they thrash out of your control.

Adopt a lower physical position to align with your child's level and engage in communication using a soft, composed tone, while ensuring consistent eye contact.

Establish limits by effectively communicating with your young child regarding the specific circumstances. It may be necessary to exercise patience until the tantrum has subsided. Establishing limits may prove to be more efficacious for older toddlers.

Ensure that the setting is infused with an element of enjoyment, while being mindful of not compromising the well-being of your children. Engage in humorous facial expressions or vocalisations, or perform an activity that you are aware your youngster finds enjoyable.

Engage in interactive communication with your child to validate their emotions and support them in effectively articulating their feelings. It is important to acknowledge and validate the emotions of individuals who may be experiencing distress or dissatisfaction, reassuring them that such sentiments are valid and permissible.

Emphasize the implications of your child's actions: "Mary began to weep when you hit her." "It was painful. She was both depressed and furious." "She no longer wanted to play with you, which made you sad."

Consider what better choice(s) your child might make the next time. "What other options do you have if Mary takes the little truck you're playing with?" If your child has no ideas (which is very typical), you might recommend some tactics, such as encouraging them to use their words: "That is my truck." "Please return it, and then offer Mary another vehicle."Remind your child that they can still turn to you for assistance.

After you've given them a few suggestions, they may be able to come up with some on their own. The willingness to substitute an appropriate action for a non-acceptable action is a critical component of developing self-control. It is also a valuable ability for succeeding in school and life. Bear in It should be noted that the optimal timing for engaging in the brainstorming process may differ depending on the individual child. There are those who may derive advantages by engaging in immediate contemplation on the matter subsequent to the occurrence. In contrast, others need more time to cool down and be more open to this phase later.Here are few alternative strategies that may potentially mitigate rage in toddlers:

It is advisable to adhere to a consistent regimen to the greatest extent feasible.

It is advisable to proactively anticipate and strategize for any modifications in the routine or surroundings of a toddler. In situations where there are last-minute changes to plans or unexpected deviations from the original plan, it is advisable to retain a positive mindset. This will facilitate the modelling of desired habits in your youngster.

Facilitate the development of emotional expression in young children by employing strategies such as expanding their language or teaching them coping mechanisms like stomping.

When faced with a challenge, it is advisable to provide assistance to toddlers in order to facilitate their problem-solving abilities.

When a youngster demonstrates positive behaviour, it is advisable to provide them with positive reinforcement.

It is advisable to refrain from subjecting one's child to situations that may cause discomfort or unease, as well as from providing them with toys that beyond their developmental capabilities.

One can mitigate the occurrence of violent outbursts by exercising emotional regulation.

Holding the expectation that one's child will consistently experience happiness is an impractical notion, as toddlers, akin to all individuals, undergo a range of emotions. Engage in a conversation with your child regarding their emotional state and assist them in comprehending the complex array of emotions they are currently encountering.

It is acknowledged that there was a time when we occupied the role of such parents - namely, the most industrious and anxiety-ridden parents globally. It was only when we adopted a disregard for the opinions of others and embraced a minimalist lifestyle that our circumstances started to improve. The primary constituents around which our daily agenda is constructed encompass three elements:

What are the top three to five priorities for today? Each individual proceeds to document the information in written form.

The principle of "less is more" suggests that simplicity and minimalism can often be more effective and desirable. Conversely, the principle of "more is less" implies that an excess of something might diminish its value or impact. The notion of multitasking is often regarded as a fallacy, thus suggesting that individuals should not concern themselves with attempting to engage in multiple tasks simultaneously and instead focus on maintaining a positive and contented mindset.

Implementing our priorities. In the course of one's existence, unexpected challenges are bound to arise. However, when all matters are regarded as equally important, the concept of priority becomes diluted and loses its significance.

All other additions are evaluated in relation to these three fundamental daily objectives.

One recommended course of action

Engage in introspection: What activities may one reduce in frequency on a daily basis, so allowing for a greater degree of parental satisfaction?

An Examination of Anger Management Patterns

Individuals who were raised in an atmosphere characterised by inadequate anger management may have internalised similar behavioural patterns. The emotion of anger can be observed to persist across multiple generations. In the absence of underlying mental health conditions, it is widely acknowledged among mental health professionals that anger is predominantly acquired via the process of learning. Consequently, it is common for individuals to attribute their angry characteristics to a familial influence, such as their father, mother, sibling, or grandparent, who exhibited negative manifestations of anger.

It is important to recall that we have previously established the notion that all emotions, including rage, are anticipated. Nevertheless, the expression of anger through harmful means, such as raising one's voice and engaging in shouting, is generally regarded as undesirable. Typically, the child's family imparts knowledge regarding appropriate responses to experienced emotions. Similarly, one's response to anger may be an inherent approach mechanism.

While certain individuals adopted a strategy of internalising their emotions, others recognised that a vehement outburst of vocalisations served as the most effective means of conveying their rage. Regardless, it is evident that upon identifying the anger management patterns prevalent within your familial context, you possess the agency to disrupt this detrimental cycle. Consequently, you have the capacity to make a conscious decision to refrain from perpetuating these patterns to subsequent generations, so safeguarding your children from inheriting such behaviours.

A suggestion for doing action

Contemplate: Is rage prevalent throughout your familial lineage? Is it possible for an individual to identify a family member who has displayed a particular characteristic? Describe the response of the individual to intense anger. Did this person suppress their emotions until there was a significant outburst? Reaffirm your determination to deviate from the individual's chosen trajectory.

The underlying factors contributing to the manifestation of anger from a structural perspective.

The experience of structural fury frequently arises from a sense of being inundated or experiencing high levels of stress. This phenomenon might arise due to various circumstances, such as financial constraints, occupational pressures, or an overwhelming workload. When an individual is already experiencing a high level of stress and demands, it requires less effort from a toddler to exacerbate the situation and cause the individual to reach a breaking point. Toddlers can provide challenges in several situations, such as exhibiting disruptive behaviour in public or resisting bedtime routines. However, on certain occasions, individuals may experience stress unrelated to their child, yet inadvertently direct their frustration towards them.

Regardless of the underlying factors contributing to one's anger, it is crucial to recognise that frequently succumbing to anger towards a young child can have detrimental effects on the parent-child relationship, potentially instilling fear within the child. If an individual is experiencing difficulty in maintaining a state of calmness, a simple technique to assist in regulating anger is to engage in deep breathing exercises while simultaneously counting to 10. One may also consider temporarily disengaging from the situation for a brief period, allowing oneself the opportunity to regain composure.

If, subsequent to the implementation of this strategy, one continues to experience feelings of anger, it is advisable to engage in a conversation with a trusted individual, such as a friend or family member, in order to address and discuss these emotions. The act of suppressing one's anger has the potential to exacerbate its negative effects over an extended period of time. Although it is natural for parents to experience anger on occasion, it is crucial to make an effort to manage and regulate this emotion for the well-being of their child.

As seen from the present discourse, mitigating the trajectory of rage necessitates a more substantial commitment than a mere transient desire. It is advisable to allocate a sufficient amount of time for engaging in introspective practises. Engage in self-reflection to get insight into the underlying motivations that drive your behaviour. Next, proceed with the gradual implementation of solutions. The process of overcoming mistakes necessitates a steadfast commitment to consistently exerting maximum effort in order to extricate ourselves from challenging situations. In order to provide support and discourage resignation, it is necessary to examine the ramifications of anger on one's offspring.

3. Determining the origin of one's anger

One important aspect of utilising anger in a constructive manner involves the identification of the underlying cause or origin of one's anger. It is important to use caution in order to avoid conflating the concept of cause with that of source. The origin of one's rage consistently stems from within oneself. Gaining awareness of one's personal role in the experience of rage might facilitate the acquisition of effective strategies for anger management.

Do you recall the individual named Amy? The individual has recently acknowledged that her colleague, Pascal, consistently exhibits disrespectful behaviour towards her, which elicits feelings of anger inside her. Prior to engaging in a confrontation, the individual in question has refrained from directly addressing the subject of her discontent. Instead, she has chosen to undertake the task of discerning the root cause of her emotional turmoil. Upon careful consideration, Amy has come to the belief that the reason for her dissatisfaction is rooted in the lack of proper treatment and respect accorded to her. The reason behind her anger can be attributed to Pascal's behaviour, while the origin of her anger, which stems from feeling insulted, is closely linked to her self-perception. In this particular instance, it might be argued that Amy's fury is warranted.

Upon acknowledging that the origin of one's anger lies inside oneself, it is conceivable that expressing the reasons for one's wrath towards another individual may become a more manageable task. It is imperative for individuals to assume accountability for their rage. This is harnessing one's anger in a constructive manner to facilitate positive transformation, rather than suppressing, repressing, or exhibiting excessive reactions to it.

Could you please provide an answer to my query?

Which sentence serves as an example of recognising the origin of one's anger?

I am experiencing frustration regarding John's advancement, as I perceive a disparity between the respect I believe I merit and the acknowledgment I am currently receiving." "The ideals exhibited by my coworkers are morally objectionable, which may contribute to my persistent feelings of anger during my time at work.

The primary source of my frustration stems from my supervisor, who, regrettably, fails to engage in meaningful dialogue with me over the matter, so exacerbating my already heightened state of anger.

The response to the user's query is as follows.

One possible option is to rewrite the user's text to be more academic in nature. This can be achieved by making the language more The option provided is deemed to be accurate. The source of one's wrath can be traced back to oneself. The experience of anger can be triggered by an external incident; nevertheless, it is important to acknowledge that one's response to this event ultimately lies within their personal responsibility.

Option 2: This alternative is deemed to be wrong. The potential for experiencing anger at the workplace can be attributed to the actions of coworkers, although it is important to note that they are not the primary cause of this emotional response. Rather, it is the individual's subjective perception that their coworkers' beliefs are in conflict with their own, leading to a sense of offence and subsequent anger.

choice 3: This particular choice is deemed to be wrong. When individuals perceive the origin of their anger as originating from external factors, they tend to absolve themselves of any personal responsibility for their emotional state.

Taking into account the alternative viewpoint

An additional crucial element in effectively harnessing anger in the workplace is the deliberate consideration of the alternative viewpoint held by the other individual involved. wrath is a subjective and often overwhelming emotional state, which can impede cognitive processes and divert attention towards the personal impact of one's wrath. The presented perspective lacks balance and fails to contribute constructively to the discourse.

In instances where one has a strong emotional response such as wrath, it is advisable to broaden one's comprehension to encompass the viewpoint of the other individual involved and contemplate the underlying motivations behind their actions. Seeking direct input from the one with whom one is experiencing anger can be an effective approach to gain a deeper comprehension of their perspective. It may be argued that the actions you have recently undertaken have elicited a strong emotional response from me, specifically anger. Could you please provide an explanation for your actions? It is important to use caution in order to avoid appearing contentious. This can be achieved by prioritising clarity, directness, and respectfulness in one's communication.

An additional approach to attain a broader perspective is empathising with the other individual by placing oneself in their situation and contemplating the potential reasons underlying their behaviour. For example, it is possible that he lacks proficiency in performing his professional duties. Alternatively, it is plausible that he lacks essential information or is experiencing significant levels of stress. Alternatively, it is plausible that he perceives your behaviour as impolite and intentionally engages in actions with the intention of provoking your wrath.

Reflect at the circumstances involving Amy and Pascal. Frequently, she experiences feelings of anger at Pascal due to his disrespectful conduct directed towards her.

Join Amy as she contemplates Pascal's perspective.

It is possible that the individual in question possesses divergent objectives in comparison to my own, leading them to perceive me as a potential source of harm or challenge.

Am I effectively portraying myself? It is plausible that I am inadvertently conveying a negative sentiment towards him, thereby eliciting a corresponding response from him.

Is there any action on my part that may have triggered his behaviour? Is there any way in which I may be inadvertently contributing to this scenario that I have failed to recognise?

Are the expectations regarding Pascal's behaviour deemed as unreasonable?

In the present scenario, it is Amy who is experiencing anger. Engaging in introspective inquiry on the underlying motivations behind Pascal's behaviour may facilitate the identification of insights that may be leveraged to channel her anger in a constructive manner.

www.ingramcontent.com/pod-product-compliance
Lightning Source LLC
Chambersburg PA
CBHW052137110526
44591CB00012B/1763